MW00532848

"Tom Pennington is a seasoned pastor and faithful ~ ¡
uncommon giftedness. His understanding of what the church is to be and
how it is to function, is true to Scripture and well presented in this book, *Three
Hallmarks of a Biblical Church Member*. I believe that every Christian would
be well served to read this book and follow its counsel. May God's church be
strengthened as its members learn what is required of them through the truth
found in these pages."

Steven J. Lawson, President, OnePassion Ministries, Teaching Fellow,
Ligonier Ministries, Professor of Preaching, The Masters Seminary

"In this meaty and satisfying book, Tom Pennington helps us love the
church better through the pursuit of meaningful membership. Meaningful
membership that makes a priority of actively attending Lord's Day worship,
discovering and deploying one's spiritual gifts for the benefit of others, and
sharing life together in loving community. In a day of church hopping and
shopping let this timely resource help you ask not what your church can do
for you but what you can do for your church."

Philip De Courcy, Pastor, Kindred Community Church (Anaheim
Hills, California) and teacher on the daily radio program *Know the
Truth*

"In this concise and penetrating look at church membership, Tom Pennington
provides a compelling biblical case for committed involvement in a local
church. He takes us from the vitality of corporate worship to the practical
dynamics of fellowship in the body, giving us fresh eyes to see the joy and
spiritual strength of active membership in a local assembly. Prepare to have
your assumptions challenged, your convictions deepened, and your usefulness
freshly invigorated."

Jerry Wragg, Senior Pastor, Grace Immanuel Bible Church (Jupiter,
Florida), President, The Expositors Seminary (Jupiter, Florida), author of *Courageous Churchmen* and co-author of *Free to Be Holy*

"In a welcomed twist on how most people think about their relationship with their church, Tom Pennington prompts Christians to take the next step and not only consider whether their church meets their expectations. God, of course, has revealed a set of expectations for every church member as well. This concise and helpful guide unpacks the essential biblical requirements which all Christians would do well to utilize as the means for prayerful reflection and self-evaluation."

Mike Fabarez, Senior Pastor, Compass Bible Church (Aliso Viejo, California)

"What Tom writes in this book represents truth that he has practiced. He has practiced these truths as a Christian, and he has taught and led others in the practice of these truths as a faithful shepherd. This is a book desperately needed at the present time. The teaching of biblical ecclesiology is sorely neglected, and the result is that believers and churches are suffering. This is a resource that I rejoice in greatly and plan to make use of in the life of our own congregation."

Richard Caldwell Jr., Pastor-Teacher, Founders Baptist Church (Spring, Texas) author of *Pastoral Preaching: Expository Preaching for Pastoral Work*

Three Hallmarks of a Biblical Church Member

TOM PENNINGTON

Three Hallmarks
of a
Biblical Church Member

WHAT CHRIST REQUIRES OF EVERY
TRUE CHRISTIAN IN HIS CHURCH

THE
Greater Heritage
Christian Publishing
Winter Springs, FL

Three Hallmarks of a Biblical Church Member by Tom Pennington
Paperback and eBook editions first published October 2022
© 2022 The Greater Heritage

Published by The Greater Heritage
   1170 Tree Swallow Dr., Suite 309
   Winter Springs, FL 32708

Email: info@thegreaterheritage.com
Website: www.thegreaterheritage.com

Cover Design: The Greater Heritage
Cover Symbols: © rawpixel ID: 599575
Font(s): Adobe Caslon Pro, Calluna, Cardo, Proforma, Objektiv Mk1, MrsEavesPetiteCaps, Vollkorn.

Library of Congress Control Number: 2022916401

ISBN (paperback): 978-1-953855-72-5
ISBN (PDF): 978-1-953855-78-7
ISBN (EPUB): 978-1-953855-76-3

1 2 3 4 5 6 7 8 9 10 26 25 24 23 22

To the members of Countryside Bible Church
whose unwavering commitment to these hallmarks
make them a delight to know and a joy to serve.

Contents

Foreword

When we consider becoming involved in a church, there are many things we are likely to evaluate. These might include the quality of the children's and youth ministries, whether they have a singles' ministry, the type of music, the quality of the sermons, the friendliness of the church, etc.

While there is nothing inherently wrong with considering the various ministries that a church has to offer when looking for a church, we must understand that it is not the various ministries that make a church biblical, but biblical church members.

In this book, Pastor Tom Pennington reminds us that we have a responsibility to consider what kind of church members we are. Far too many professing Christians approach the church as a commodity designed to benefit them, without any consideration of their biblical responsibility to the church. This consumer mentality has created churches that simply do not reflect biblical priorities.

Tom presents a case for three biblical "hallmarks" of a church member. Each hallmark is defined and defended by the Scripture. While explaining these vital truths for every believer, Tom is careful to engage the reader with his or her personal obligation to live in light of these truths.

As you read this eminently practical book, reflect on your own life. Are you contributing to the body of Christ by fulfilling your personal responsibility in worship, service, and fellowship?

When all of the members of a church understand and commit to fulfill God's purposes for them in the context of the church, the benefits are immense. God is truly worshiped, believers are faithfully serving one another, the fellowship is as God intended, and the world can see the incredible testimony of the unified body of Christ in action.

Do you want to be a biblical church member? Carefully read this book and make it your aim to worship God, serve the body of Christ, and participate in the fellowship of the church. As we all determine to be obedient to these principles in God's word, the church becomes what God intends it to be.

To God be the glory!

Rocky Wyatt
Executive Director
XL Ministries, Inc.
xlministries.org

Introduction

In the twelfth century, the Worshipful Company of Goldsmiths was founded in London. Their main function was analyzing and testing precious metals such as gold, silver and platinum. In 1300, King Edward I passed a statute that created and enforced precise regulations concerning the genuineness and purity of gold and silver. Because of this, the Goldsmith's Hall—as it's more commonly known—was legally and formally recognized in Britain. The Goldsmith's Hall received its first royal charter in 1327. Due to its expertise in the metals industry and influence both locally and worldwide, the Goldsmith's Hall was eventually established as one of the Twelve Great Livery Companies.

By 1363, after costly metals were rigorously tested and the standard for purity was approved, goldsmiths and silversmiths alike were mandated to mark their metals with an official stamp. When the Goldsmith's Hall stamped its mark on a piece of metal it was said to have received the *hallmark*, confirming the metal had passed a series of meticulous tests. The Goldsmith's Hall and its unique branding is the origin of the English word *hallmark*. As time passed and the linguistic usage of *hallmark* expanded, it came to be used to describe anything that met a certain standard of excellence.

Tragically, many Christians today wouldn't receive a hallmark for being a biblical church member—they fail to meet the Scriptural standards. What is equally true, I fear, is that a great number of Christians have no idea what it even means to be a biblical member of Christ's church. They either attend, or have come from, churches where the Word of God isn't a priority and have never been taught from Scripture how to be a biblical church member.

A related problem is that some Christians think about church in the same way they think about a restaurant: they choose one based on their tastes and preferences, only go when they desire, order what they wish, have all their wants and needs met, and then leave without any sense of responsibility to their fellow diners or the establishment. That kind of thinking may fit your experience at a restaurant, but it's certainly not how one ought to conduct himself in the "household of God" (1 Tim. 3:15).

In the twentieth century, Martyn Lloyd-Jones warned the church of this very danger when he wrote, "The central error of modern thinking, surely, is that today men and women imagine they have the right to decide for themselves, anew and afresh, what Christianity is, what the church is, and what her message is."[1] Lloyd-Jones recognized the devastating impact of defining the church apart from God's Word. As followers of Christ, we cannot neglect what the Scripture says is required of us in the local church. The way we

---

1 Martyn Lloyd-Jones, *Authentic Christianity: Studies in the Book of Acts*, vol. 1 (Wheaton, IL: Crossway, 2000), 187.

function in the church truly matters.

The New Testament compares the church to a human body, and individual Christians are members of that body with a function to fulfill and a role to perform (1 Cor. 12:12ff). Romans 12:5 says, "So we, who are many, are one body in Christ, and individually members one of another."

The church is also described as a family. The apostle John writes, "See how great a love the Father has bestowed on us, that we would be called children of God; and *such* we are" (1 John 3:1). Paul adds, "While we have opportunity, let us do good to all people, and especially to those who are of the household of the faith" (Gal. 6:10). Christians belong to a family, just as we belong to our earthly families. That means you and I have obligations both to the head of the family—God the Father—and to our brothers and sisters in Christ.

For these reasons, all Christians must earnestly strive to be biblical church members. Of course, there's an extensive list of activities you can engage in as a member of a church—activities that are good and helpful in their own right. But what commitments make a biblical church member? The New Testament identifies three primary hallmarks of a biblical church member: You must engage in corporate worship by committing to exalt God with your church on the Lord's Day. You must actively serve in your church using the spiritual gifts God has given you. And you must engage in true fellowship—that is, loving and caring for the rest of the members in your church.

These are the three primary hallmarks that identify a genuine New Testament church member. They are at the heart of what it means to be a biblical member of Christ's church. Everyone who belongs to the body of Christ must pursue these hallmarks.

Hallmark #1

Corporate Worship

Let the word of Christ richly dwell within you, with all wisdom teaching and admonishing one another with psalms and hymns and spiritual songs, singing with thankfulness in your hearts to God.

COLOSSIANS 3:16

ONE

Worship in the Church

In his book *For the Glory of God: Recovering a Biblical Theology of Worship*, Daniel I. Block writes, "Evangelicals must rediscover that the goal of congregational worship and all of ministry is the glory of God, and that God the Father and God the Son are most glorified when we sing of them and not of ourselves."[1] Block is right. We must recapture the biblical purpose and goal of corporate worship. This is necessary for a church to be biblical, and it's a nonnegotiable part of being a biblical member. The first hallmark of a biblical church member is that you participate in corporate worship that's rooted in Scripture and exalts God.

What Is Worship?

The English word *worship* comes from the Anglo-Saxon word "weorthscipe." In modern English it literally reads *worth-ship*, and

---

1 Daniel I. Block, *For the Glory of God: Recovering a Biblical Theology of Worship* (Grand Rapids: Baker, 2014), 237.

it means to acknowledge the quality or condition of worth in God. Worship is to recognize the worthiness, dignity and merit of God and to pay Him the respect or homage that's His right. The *International Standard Bible Encyclopedia* defines worship this way: "Worship is an exercise of the human spirit that is directed primarily to God. It is an enterprise undertaken not simply to satisfy our need or to make us feel better or to minister to our aesthetic taste or social well-being, but to express the worthiness of God Himself."[2] In other words, worship is seeing and savoring the worthiness of God and responding as He deserves.

What is the key idea behind biblical worship? The Scripture reveals that worship is always, without exception, a response to God and His self-revelation. It has been rightly said that to know God is to worship Him. When people encounter the one true God of the Bible, they always respond in worship. Even His enemies are forced to bow the knee.

When the children of Israel heard of God's compassion for them and that He freed them from the slavery and bondage in Egypt, they worshiped. Exodus 4:31 says, "So the people believed; and when they heard that the LORD was concerned about the sons of Israel and that He had seen their affliction, then they bowed low and worshiped."

After Solomon's prayer of dedication for the temple, the Lord responded by sending fire from heaven and manifesting His glory in the temple. 2 Chronicles 7:3 records the Israelites' reaction:

> All the sons of Israel, seeing the fire come down and the glory
> of the LORD upon the house, bowed down on the pavement
> with their faces to the ground, and they worshiped and gave

---

2 Geoffrey W. Bromiley, ed., *International Standard Bible Encyclopedia*, vol. 4, rev. ed. (Grand Rapids: Eerdmans, 1998), 1131.

praise to the LORD, *saying*, 'Truly, He is good, truly His lovingkindness [steadfast love] is everlasting.'

The sons of Israel saw a visible demonstration of the glory of God—the Shekinah glory. And what was their response? As the fire of God fell from the heavens, the people responded in worship. They were driven to worship because of God's self-revelation.

The book of Nehemiah also describes the people of God worshiping in response to God's self-revelation *in the Scripture*. Nehemiah 8:6 says, "Ezra blessed the LORD the great God. And all the people answered, 'Amen, Amen!' while lifting up their hands; then they bowed low and worshiped the LORD with *their* faces to the ground." Likewise, in Nehemiah 9:3, when the people saw God on the pages of Scripture, they fell down and worshiped: "While they stood in their place, they read from the book of the law of the LORD their God for a fourth of the day; and for *another* fourth they confessed and worshiped the LORD their God."

In the New Testament, the same pattern of worship given to God the Father is also given to His Son, our Lord Jesus Christ. The Gospel of Matthew records the disciples' response to Jesus miraculously walking on water and calming the storm: "Those who were in the boat worshiped Him, saying, 'You are certainly God's Son!'" (Matt. 14:33). Similarly, when Jesus appeared to His disciples after His resurrection, they fell down and worshiped. Matthew 28:9 says, "Behold, Jesus met them and greeted them. And they came up and took hold of His feet and worshiped Him." The disciples saw the glorified, risen Lord, and they fell at His feet and worshiped.

Wayne Grudem writes, "Genuine worship is not something that is self-generated or that can be worked up within ourselves. It must rather be the outpouring of our hearts in response to a realization of who God is."[3] Worship isn't an emotion that you stir up inside yourself. Rather, worship is our reasonable and normal response to a glimpse of the glory of the infinite being of God. Worship, then, is theocentric, God-centered. It's a response to either a visible display of the glory of God, or a greater understanding of who God is from His Word. Our only reasonable response to Him is worship (Rom. 12:1–2). Because we only come to know God through his Word, it's imperative for Scripture to be prominent in corporate worship, our collective response to God.

Tragically, modern worship is often defined and characterized by emotion. While it's true that emotion is involved in worship, emotion in and of itself isn't worship. People express emotion all the time. Attend a sporting event and you will see a wide range of emotions, but none of them will be worship. The foundation of biblical worship isn't our emotions; rather, worship is built on a correct knowledge of God. Therefore, our worship can only go as high as our knowledge of God is deep. They are inextricably tied together. John MacArthur writes, "The person who would worship God must therefore have a faithful commitment to the Word of God."[4] Block adds, "The integrity of worship depends upon the clarity of the divine revelation and the level of our understanding of God's will."[5]

Worship, then, is a response to the glory of God and His Word. It's only as you see Him that you will truly worship. It's possible to get emotional without God and His Word, but you cannot truly worship apart from the clear revelation of Him in His Word.

What is Corporate Worship?

In the sixteenth century, the Westminster Assembly composed a

---

3 Wayne Grudem, *Systematic Theology*, 2nd ed. (Grand Rapids: Zondervan, 2020), 1244.
4 John MacArthur, *Worship: The Ultimate Priority* (Chicago, IL: Moody, 2012), 164.
5 Block, *For the Glory of God*, 190.

document known as the *Westminster Shorter Catechism*. The leaders insisted on cataloging key elements of the Christian faith for teaching and equipping purposes. The famous first question and answer are: "What is the chief end of man? Man's chief end is to glorify God, and to enjoy him forever."[6] After a thorough examination of the Scriptures, worship was identified as the greatest priority for the Christian life and the church (see 1 Cor. 10:31; Rom. 11:36).

What does it mean to worship corporately? The word *corporate* refers to a united or collective group, or something done jointly. Corporate worship, then, is collective, joint worship. It's an entire local church joining together in worship, in seeing and savoring the worthiness of God, and responding to Him as He deserves.

Scripture is clear that worship can and must happen individually. True believers don't just worship corporately on Sunday—they also worship individually throughout the week. The pattern of Scripture is that Christians worship privately and individually. But Scripture is equally clear that all true worshipers will also engage in corporate worship. You cannot be a true worshiper individually and not be a true worshiper corporately. According to God's Word, that's an impossibility! We will examine why in the next chapter.

---

6 *Westminster Confession of Faith* (Glasgow, Scotland: Free Presbyterian, 1995), 287.

TWO

The Priority of Corporate Worship

What are the greatest priorities of your life? As we discover what the Scripture teaches, we learn that one of life's greatest priorities is corporate worship. There are a number of biblical reasons for the priority of corporate worship. But I'm confident that two primary reasons will compel you to make corporate worship a major priority in your life.

Jesus' Practice of Corporate Worship

The first reason to make corporate worship a priority in your life is our Lord's weekly practice. Jesus was committed to the Old Testament priority of corporate worship on the weekly Sabbath. In fact, a crucial part of Jesus' life and ministry was being in the synagogue on the Sabbath, corporately worshiping with God's people.

The Gospel of Luke records many examples of Jesus participating in corporate worship. He made it His habit to teach in the synagogues.

Luke 4:14–15 says, "Jesus returned to Galilee in the power of the Spirit, and news about Him spread through all the surrounding district. And He *began* teaching in their synagogues and was praised by all." The focus of Jesus' ministry was teaching in the synagogues—"it was His custom" (Luke 4:16). Weekly He attended the synagogue on the Sabbath for corporate worship.

What did corporate worship look like for Jesus? Luke 4 provides a blueprint for Jesus' involvement in corporate worship. Luke records that Jesus stood up to read in the synagogue, and the scroll of the prophet Isaiah was handed to Him (v. 16–17). When He found the place where the prophecy about Himself was written, He read it to the congregation (v. 17–19; Isa. 61:1–2a). Afterward, "He closed the book, gave it back to the attendant and sat down; and the eyes of all were fixed on Him" (v. 20). Then, verse 21 says, "*And He began to say to them*, 'Today this Scripture has been fulfilled in your hearing'" (emphasis added). This is an example of Jesus' ministry in the synagogues. He attended weekly worship on the Sabbath, and He did what was typically done in synagogues across the land: He read the text of Scripture, and then He explained it—Jesus was an expository preacher!

After the people of Nazareth rejected Him (v. 28–30), Jesus continued His ministry in the synagogues in Galilee (v. 31), then He traveled to the synagogues in Capernaum and Judea (v. 31; 44). A close look at Jesus' ministry reveals a pattern of preaching and teaching. He taught not only during the week—some of His most famous sermons on the Sea of Galilee or at the temple were taught then. But He also preached regularly in the synagogues on the Sabbath.

The primary focus of Jesus' ministry week in and week out was preaching in the synagogues on the Sabbath to the people of God when they gathered for corporate worship. From the very beginning of His life, Jesus fulfilled the Old Testament by participating in weekly corporate worship. That was the pattern of His earthly life and ministry. And it should be for us who are disciples as well.

The New Testament Church's Pattern of Corporate Worship

A second reason corporate worship must be a priority for every Christian is the pattern of the New Testament church. Under the Mosaic Covenant, the weekly day of worship was the Sabbath, or Saturday. However, that began to change beginning with the resurrection of our Lord. According to all four Gospels, He was raised from the dead on Sunday, the first day of the week (Matt. 28:1; Mark 16:2; Luke 24:1; John 20:1).

On the very night of His resurrection, Jesus appeared to ten of His disciples in the upper room. What was their response to seeing the risen Christ? They worshiped! The following Sunday, He appeared to them again, including Thomas, and they ate together and worshiped (John 20:24–29). So, a clear pattern of corporate worship on Sunday began in the earliest weeks after Jesus' resurrection.

After Jesus' ascension, believers continued to gather on Sunday for weekly worship. There's unassailable evidence of this in the New Testament. Acts 20:7 says, "On the first day of the week, when we were gathered together to break bread, Paul *began* talking to them, intending to leave the next day, and he prolonged his message until midnight." This is very similar to what God's people were doing in Acts 2. There they were meeting to receive instruction from the Word, to fellowship, and to participate in the Lord's Table and offer prayers (v. 42). In Acts 20, the believers in Troas took of the Lord's Table and listened to Paul deliver a sermon from the Scripture on Sunday. That is the first official New Testament record of Christians gathering for worship on the Lord's Day, occurring sometime in the late 50s A.D. Undoubtedly, it had happened before, but this is the first time it's recorded in Scripture.

Acts 20 wasn't a special event, nor an anomaly due to the presence of the apostle Paul. Consider Paul's directions to the Corinthians regarding giving and collecting money for churches and people in need. He writes,

> Now concerning the collection for the saints, as I directed the churches of Galatia, so do you also. On the first day of every week each one of you is to put aside and save, as he may prosper, so that no collections be made when I come. (1 Cor. 16:1–2)

Paul's command here provides insight into the worship of the early church. He says that Christians gathered together "on the *first day* of *every* week" (emphasis added). According to Paul, there was a weekly gathering on Sunday in Corinth. Who was there? Paul says "each of you" (v. 2). Every believer in Corinth gathered with one another on the Lord's Day for corporate worship.

This pattern was not unique to the church in Corinth; it also included the churches Paul had planted in the Galatian region (v. 1). And it didn't happen randomly or spontaneously. Paul says, "I *directed* the churches of Galatia" (emphasis added). The implication is that all the churches were given apostolic direction to meet every Sunday.

As a result of Jesus' resurrection, the Old Testament Sabbath worship was officially set aside. Paul makes this point in Colossians 2 when he writes,

> Therefore no one is to act as your judge in regard to food or drink or in respect to a festival or a new moon or a Sabbath

day—things which are a *mere* shadow of what is to come; but the substance belongs to Christ. (Col. 2:16–17)

In the Old Testament, every time the words *festival, new moon,* and *Sabbath* occur together, the weekly Sabbath is in view. So, when Paul uses these three expressions, he intends to show that Christians are no longer required to keep the weekly Sabbath. Why? Because it was merely a "shadow" of what was to come: our Lord Jesus Christ.

How should we respond to the reality that Christ has come into the world? The author of Hebrews describes what our response should be:

Therefore, brethren, since we have confidence to enter the holy place by the blood of Jesus, by a new and living way which He inaugurated for us through the veil, that is, His flesh, and since *we have* a great priest over the house of God, let us draw near with a sincere heart in full assurance of faith, having our hearts sprinkled *clean* from an evil conscience and our bodies washed with pure water. Let us hold fast the confession of our hope without wavering, for He who promised is faithful; and let us consider how to stimulate one another to love and good deeds, not forsaking our own assembling together, as is the habit of some, but encouraging *one another*; and all the more as you see the day drawing near. (Heb. 10:18–25)

The writer of Hebrews says that since we have been saved by the blood of Christ, we can enter into God's presence through Christ (v. 19–20). How is this possible? Because Christ is our Great High Priest, and He has given us access to the Father. In addition, the author of Hebrews gives three exhortations for every Christian: First, we must draw near to God with full confidence that we have access to Him (v. 22). Second, we must continue to persevere in the faith (v. 23). Third, we must stimulate one another to love and good deeds, as we consistently gather with one another for corporate worship (v. 24–25).

As a result of our salvation, and because Christ is our Great High Priest, we must turn our attention to our fellow Christians. In other words, don't be selfishly consumed with your own individual salvation. We ought to praise God for our own salvation, but we shouldn't be so preoccupied with it that we neglect fellowship with God's people. According to Hebrews, when the church assembles for corporate worship every Sunday, we best "stimulate one another to love and good deeds" (v. 25).

Of course, that doesn't mean we can never miss a single church service. Instead, the author of Hebrews is emphasizing the importance of *regularly* meeting for corporate worship. The Greek word for "forsaking" means "to abandon" or "desert." In context, many Jews who had professed faith in Christ were tempted to abandon their profession and go back to temple worship. The writer of Hebrews pleads with them and commands them not to abandon or forsake the corporate assembly.

That means we cannot be "Christmas and Easter only" Christians or just come to church whenever we feel like it. Rather, we must commit to weekly attendance at a biblical church because that's the pattern of both the Lord Jesus Himself and the New Testament believers. And it must be the pattern of your Christian life and experience.

In the book of Revelation, written in the late 90s AD, the apostle John makes an interesting statement regarding Sunday, the day the church is supposed to gather. He writes,

> I, John, your brother and fellow partaker in the tribulation
> and kingdom and perseverance *which are* in Jesus, was on
> the island called Patmos because of the word of God and the
> testimony of Jesus. I was in the Spirit on the Lord's day (Rev.
> 1:9–10)

The apostle John refers to Sunday as "the Lord's day."[1] What does
he mean by that title? He's declaring that Sunday, the day of corporate worship, belongs to the Lord.[2]

Therefore, Sunday should be the most important day in your
week. Why? Because it's the Lord's Day—it belongs to Him. And your
number one priority on Sunday is corporate worship. That was the
New Testament church's view of corporate worship on Sunday—and
it should be our view as well.

Substitutes for Corporate Worship

It's a common temptation for Christians to replace corporate worship with things that aren't biblical substitutes. For example, many
parachurch ministries are extremely useful to the church. For many
years it was my joy to work at Grace to You, the ministry of John
MacArthur, a parachurch ministry that helps church members grow
in their knowledge and understanding of Scripture, and in their
involvement in the local church. There's nothing inherently wrong
with parachurch ministries, but they are never a replacement for
corporate worship.

---

[1] A similar expression is found in 1 Cor. 11:20: "the Lord's Supper."
[2] "Quite possibly, this is the first use of this name for Sunday in Christian history. If so,
it began a habit picked up by other Christian writers shortly after John's time." Robert L.
Thomas, *Revelation 1–7*, An Exegetical Commentary (Chicago, IL: Moody, 1992), 91.

Some argue that a home Bible study or a Sunday school class replaces the church. Others argue that a radio, television, or internet preacher can replace the local church. A more recent substitute is the online streaming of church services. Of course, being able to stream a church service is a wonderful resource, especially if people are sick or happen to be traveling. The internet also provides many other helpful tools that can feed your soul if you are still hungry for God's Word. However, streaming and other online resources aren't viable substitutes for the biblical requirement of corporate worship.

The New Testament heavily prioritizes corporate worship. Why is it so important? Because we belong to God's family, and to focus solely on individual worship is practically to say: "I am the only one of God's children who really matters to Him." In fact, refusing to participate in corporate worship is a failure to love others as you love yourself, and, therefore, a failure to love God (Matt. 22:34–40). 1 John 4:19–20 says, "We love because He [God] first loved us. If someone says, 'I love God,' and hates his brother, he is a liar; for the one who does not love his brother whom he has seen, cannot love God whom he has not seen." The apostle John says if you don't love God's people, you don't love God—you love yourself. John goes on to say, "This commandment we have from Him, that the one who loves God should love his brother also" (4:21). If you treat church like a restaurant where you come and go as you please without any obligation to others, you prove that you don't really love God, because you don't love His people.

Therefore, your participation in corporate worship reveals your love for God and His people. This is the serious nature of worshiping with other believers—it's no small matter. It's absolutely critical to the Christian life.

THREE

The Elements of Corporate Worship

As we continue to focus on what Scripture teaches about corporate worship, it's vital to identify and understand what the elements of corporate worship are. Those elements are determined by the Reformation principle known as *sola Scriptura*, or Scripture alone, which states that the Bible is the ultimate authority for everything in our faith and practice. The Reformers of the sixteenth century universally agreed on the basic principle of *sola Scriptura*, but they didn't agree on how it ought to govern the elements of corporate worship.

The Lutherans and Anglicans joined the Roman Catholics in embracing the *normative principle*, which teaches that anything Scripture doesn't explicitly forbid is acceptable in corporate worship. In other words, the normative principle asks: does Scripture forbid this practice in worship? If Scripture doesn't say it's wrong, then it's permissible in corporate worship.

The opposing principle of worship born out of the Reformation is known as the *regulative principle*. This principle teaches that only the activities Scripture explicitly prescribes are acceptable in worship. John Calvin, who affirmed the regulative principle, writes, "God disapproves of all modes of worship not expressly sanctioned by His word."[1] The regulative principle teaches that if the Bible doesn't explicitly say to worship God in a particular way, it isn't permissible in corporate worship.

This was the prevailing opinion of biblical pastors and scholars during the Reformation. *The Westminster Confession of Faith*, representing Presbyterian thought, says,

> The acceptable way of worshiping the true God is instituted by Himself, and so limited by His own revealed will, that He may not be worshiped according to the imaginations and devices of men, or the suggestions of Satan, under any visible representation, or any other way not prescribed in the holy Scripture.[2]

The *1689 Baptist Confession of Faith*, captures the Baptist perspective,

> The acceptable way of worshiping the true God is instituted by himself and so limited by his own revealed will, that he may not be worshiped according to the imagination and devices of men, nor the suggestions of Satan, under any visible representations, or any other way not prescribed in the Holy

---

1 John Calvin, "The Necessity of Reforming the Church," in *Calvin's Tracts Relating to the Reformation*, vol. 1 (Edinburgh: Calvin Translation Society, 1844), 128.

2 *The Westminster Confession of Faith* (Glasgow, Scotland: Free Presbyterian, 1995), 89–90.

Scriptures.[3]

If it cannot be found in Scripture, it ought not be done.

Hughes Oliphant Old writes, "The basic acts of worship we perform because they are clearly commanded in Scripture. The ways and means of doing them, we try to order according to Scriptural principles."[4] Scripture leaves no room for error when it comes to the worship of God. This is stated most clearly in the Second Commandment, which says, "You shall not make for yourself an idol, or any likeness of what is in heaven above or on the earth beneath or in the water under the earth. You shall not worship them or serve them" (Exod. 20:4–5). Not only does this commandment strictly forbid the use of idols, but it also describes how unprescribed forms of worship soon become idolatry. A. W. Pink writes:

> The first commandment points out the one only object of worship; the second [commandment] tells us *how* He is to be worshipped—in spirit and in truth, by faith and not by images which appeal to the senses. The design of this commandment is to draw us away from carnal conceptions of God and to prevent His worship being profaned by superstitious rites.[5]

In Exodus 32, the golden calf was meant to symbolize the true God. After Aaron completed it, he called for "a feast to the LORD" (Exod. 32:5). However, it led the Israelites to worship Him in an

---

3 Samuel E. Waldron, *A Modern Exposition of the 1689 Baptist Confession of Faith* (Durham, England: Evangelical Press, 1989), 264.

4 Hughes Oliphant Old, *Worship*, rev. ed. (Louisville, KY: Westminster John Knox, 2002), 172.

5 A.W. Pink, *Gleanings in Exodus* (Chicago, IL: Moody, 1981), 162.

unsanctioned manner. Their failure to worship Him as He had prescribed actually obscured the glory of God.

Human ideas for worship may look like worship and may be emotionally compelling, but they don't please God. The further we step away from what Scripture prescribes, the less we actually worship.

Therefore, our corporate worship must only include these seven biblically mandated elements:

1. *Scriptural Singing*

    - "I will sing with the spirit and I will sing with the mind also" (1 Cor. 14:15b).
    - "Speaking to one another in psalms and hymns and spiritual songs, singing and making melody with your heart to the Lord" (Eph. 5:19).
    - "Let the word of Christ richly dwell within you, with all wisdom teaching and admonishing one another with psalms *and* hymns *and* spiritual songs, singing with thankfulness in your hearts to God" (Col. 3:16).

2. *Scriptural Prayer*

    - "First of all, then, I urge that entreaties *and* prayers, petitions *and* thanksgivings, be made on behalf of all men" (1 Tim. 2:1).

    - "Therefore I want the men in every place to pray, lifting up holy hands, without wrath and dissension" (1 Tim. 2:8).

3. *Scripture Reading*

- "Until I come, give attention to the *public reading of Scripture*, to exhortation and teaching" (1 Tim. 4:13).

4. *Scriptural Teaching*

- "Until I come, give attention to the *public* reading of Scripture, *to exhortation and teaching*" (1 Tim. 4:13).

- "I solemnly charge *you* in the presence of God and of Christ Jesus, who is to judge the living and the dead, and by His appearing and His kingdom: *preach the word*; be ready in season *and* out of season; reprove, rebuke, exhort, with great patience and instruction" (2 Tim. 4:1-2).

5. *Scriptural Giving (Freewill Offerings)*

- "Now concerning the collection for the saints, as I directed the churches of Galatia, so do you also. On the first day of every week each one of you is to put aside and save, as he may prosper, so that no collections be made when I come" (1 Cor. 16:1–2).

- "I testify that according to their ability, and beyond their ability, *they gave* of their own accord" (2 Cor. 8:3).

- "Each one *must do* just as he has purposed in his heart, not grudgingly or under compulsion, for God loves a cheerful giver" (2 Cor. 9:7).

- "You yourselves also know, Philippians, that at the first preaching of the gospel, after I left Macedonia, no church shared with me in the matter of giving and receiving but you alone; for even in Thessalonica you sent *a gift* more than once for my needs" (Phil. 4:15–16).

6. *Believer's Baptism*

- "Go therefore and make disciples of all the nations, baptizing them in the name of the Father and the Son and the Holy Spirit, teaching them to observe all that I commanded you; and lo, I am with you always, even to the end of the age" (Matt. 28:19–20).

- "So then, those who had received his word were baptized; and that day there were added about three thousand souls" (Acts 2:41).

- "Crispus, the leader of the synagogue, believed in the Lord with all his household, and many of the Corinthians when they heard were believing and being baptized" (Acts 18:8).

7. *The Lord's Table*

- "I received from the Lord that which I also delivered to you, that the Lord Jesus in the night in which He was betrayed took bread; and when He had given thanks, He broke it and said, 'This is My body, which is for you; do this in remembrance of Me.' In the same way *He took* the cup also after supper, saying, 'This cup is the new covenant in My blood; do this, as often as you drink *it*, in remembrance of Me.' For as often as you eat this bread and drink the cup, you proclaim the Lord's death until He comes" (1 Cor. 11:23–26).

Those seven elements reflect the regulative principle because they come directly from the Word of God. Therefore, they stand as the only legitimate way to worship God. Carl Trueman writes, "Worship that is true will focus on these trends: The Word read, the Word sung, the Word prayed, the Word seen (in the sacraments), and the Word preached. We owe these things to God's people—more importantly to God himself."[6] Churches must adhere to these divine directives without adding to them. Conducting worship according to this principle certainly adds solemnity to corporate worship, but it also brings us great joy. When we do these things with sincerity and clean hands and pure hearts, we can be confident that God is pleased. We honor God by doing in worship exactly as He has commanded us.

---

6 Carl R. Trueman, *Reformation: Yesterday, Today and Tomorrow* (Scotland, United Kingdom: Christian Focus, 2000), 138.

FOUR

The Practice of Corporate Worship

We have discovered that attending corporate worship must be a weekly priority for every true believer—that's a nonnegotiable hallmark of a biblical church member. But that invites the crucial question: what are *you* supposed to do when you attend corporate worship? It isn't enough to make sure your body shows up on Sunday. The fact that you are filling a seat doesn't mean you have worshiped God. In reality, the practice of corporate worship requires two intentional commitments.

Commit to Worship from Your Heart

First, you must deliberately engage in individual worship from your heart. When we come together for corporate worship, it starts with each of us. If each individual isn't worshiping, there's no worship. Worship begins in the heart of every person. Jesus affirmed this in John 4:24 when He says to the Samaritan woman, "God is spirit, and those who worship Him must worship in spirit and truth." Jesus is teaching because God is spirit and doesn't have a body, we must worship Him in our own spirit.

In John 4:24, Jesus adds that the true worshiper must worship "in truth." That means, first, our worship must be directed to the true God revealed in Scripture. There's no true worship if it's directed anywhere besides the God of the Bible. Second, we must worship God based on the complete revelation of Scripture. Scripture alone must inform our worship. To worship God "in truth" we must worship Him solely according to the biblical revelation of both who He is and how He desires to be worshiped.

To worship *in spirit* means we must worship from within, from our souls. A.W. Pink writes,

> To worship spiritually is the opposite of mere external rites which pertained to the flesh; instead, it is to give to God the homage of an enlightened mind and an affectionate heart. To worship Him is to worship Him according to the Truth, in a manner suited to the revelation He has made of Himself; and, no doubt, it also carries with it the force of worshiping truly, not in pretense, but sincerely. Such, and such alone, are the acceptable worshipers.[1]

God has always demanded that true worship come from within. Deuteronomy 6:5–6 says, "You shall love the Lord your God with all *your heart* and with all *your soul* and with all *your might*" (emphasis added). God isn't satisfied when your body shows up. He's only pleased if your mind, soul, and heart are completely engaged in

---

[1] Arthur W. Pink, *Exposition of the Gospel of John*, vol. 1 (Grand Rapids: Zondervan, 1975), 206.

worshiping Him. This is true of all biblical obedience. Deuteronomy 26:16 says, "This day the Lord your God commands you to do these statutes and ordinances. You shall therefore be careful to do them with all your heart and with all your soul." In other words, it's only true obedience when your heart and soul are engaged.

The faithful people of God have always worshiped from the heart. King David—a man after God's own heart—wrote, "Bless the Lord, O my soul, and all that is within me, bless His holy name" (Ps. 103:1). Jesus' mother, Mary, said, "*My soul* exalts the Lord, and *my spirit* has rejoiced in God my Savior" (Luke 1:46–47; emphasis added).

To worship in spirit means that when you gather for worship, you first make a *conscious decision* to worship, and then, you make an *ongoing effort* to engage in worship. Every moment you must remind yourself that you are worshiping the God who created you and provides all things for you, the One who is your Redeemer, Savior, and friend. Your heart has to be captivated in this way.

And your heart must be actively engaged in all seven elements of worship.

When you *sing* with other believers, you ought to sing to God from your heart. That requires more than just moving your lips; it means your heart is fully engaged. It means you are sincere, authentic, and truly mean the words you are singing to your heavenly Father.

And there are no excuses not to sing, including your singing ability (or lack thereof). God doesn't care about the quality of your voice, but about the disposition of your heart. Dozens of times Scripture commands believers to sing! Put more bluntly, if you profess to be a follower of Jesus Christ and don't sing, you are being openly disobedient to God and His Word.

In *prayer*, follow the one who is leading by talking to God along with him. Agree with what the person leading the prayer is saying and express it to God yourself. Or, reword and reshape what is being prayed in your own way and offer it to God. Regardless, you must actively pray from your heart.

When your pastor or another church leader *reads the Scripture* out loud, remind yourself that this is God's Word to His people.

When you *hear the Word taught*, listen as if Christ Himself were teaching God's Word to you. To be clear, I'm not saying that you should listen to your pastor like you listen to Christ—you accept every word that Jesus Christ says in His Word! In your pastor's case you need to make sure, like the Bereans in Acts 17:11, that what he's saying reflects the true meaning of Scripture. But, once you have discerned that it's true to Scripture, you need to listen as if Christ Himself were teaching, and submit to that truth by doing what it says (Jas. 1:22).

To worship in spirit also means to *give* regularly in keeping with how God has prospered you, and do so cheerfully as to the Lord (2 Cor. 9:6–7). Use the means God has blessed you with for the support of your local church and the propagation of the gospel around the world.

Being a true worshiper means you obey Christ in believer's *baptism*. You need to be baptized, and support others who pursue baptism with your presence and encouragement.

When you take of *the Lord's Table*, you must engage your mind by confessing your sin and remembering what Jesus Christ has done for you on the cross.

Commit to Worship for the Benefit of Others

Participating in corporate worship means that you are committed to engaging in individual worship from your heart, but it also demands that you deliberately commit to join in corporate worship with, and for the benefit of, others. This aspect of corporate worship is often neglected. Worship has both a vertical focus—God—and a horizontal focus—the people around you. Although our worship is to be primarily focused on God, worship with other believers is actually a chance for us to be aware of, and minister to, the people around us. This balance between the vertical and the horizontal exists in all elements of worship. Your worship should be offered to God, but intentionally offered with and for others.

For example, when we pray corporately, pray to God. However, Jesus makes an interesting point in the Sermon on the Mount when He teaches His disciples—and us—how to pray. He says, "Give *us* this day our daily bread. And forgive *us* our debts, as we also have forgiven our debtors. And do not lead *us* into temptation, but deliver *us* from evil" (Matt. 6:11–13; emphasis added). Jesus' use of the plural pronoun "us" is often overlooked, but it's intended to deliberately emphasize the corporate aspect of prayer. Therefore, in corporate prayer you are to pray with others and for others.

Another example is when we sing in corporate worship. We sing primarily to God, but we should also sing with others and even for others. Did you know our singing is both for God and the people around us? It's an interesting concept that you may never have considered. Ephesians 5:18–19 says, "Do not get drunk with wine, for that is dissipation, but be filled with the Spirit, *speaking to one another* in psalms and hymns and spiritual songs, singing and making melody with your heart to the Lord" (emphasis added). Paul calls the believers in Ephesus to speak to one another in song (the horizontal aspect of worship). He also tells them to sing with their hearts to the Lord (the vertical aspect of worship).

Paul makes the same points to the church of Colossae. He writes, "Let the word of Christ richly dwell within you, with all wisdom *teaching and admonishing one another* with psalms *and* hymns *and* spiritual songs, singing with thankfulness in your hearts to God" (Col. 3:16, emphasis added). Paul instructs the Colossians to teach and admonish one another through song (horizontal), and he also calls them to sing unto the Lord (vertical).

When we sing, as believers, we're to express to one another what we know to be true of God and His Word. We're to show that our confidence and hope are found in the living God and His Son. We're to affirm the great truths of the gospel of Jesus Christ to one another.

The trend in Christianity today is to elevate the style of music over its substance, and personal preference over content. Occasionally, I hear someone say that they prefer contemporary music over traditional hymns, or vice versa. That type of thinking misses the point of worship altogether. We must learn to think of others in corporate worship. Even if you prefer contemporary music over traditional hymns, it's possible the person singing next to you loves hymns and they are being taught, encouraged, and strengthened in their faith by them. For that we must praise God!

I encourage you to learn to appreciate styles of music you don't prefer. Why? Throughout its history the church has always sung both old and contemporary songs. The New Testament church sang the Psalms that are in our Bible! The oldest psalm (Ps. 90) was written by Moses 1400 years before the church began, and most of the Psalms were written a thousand years before the church age. The New Testament church also sang contemporary Christological hymns, fragments of which can be found in the New Testament (John 1:1–17; Phil. 2:6–11; Col. 1:15–20).

Historically, the church has had a rich legacy of music that has been faithfully passed from generation to generation. Our Lord intends for the church to benefit from this profound heritage.

Would You Receive the Hallmark?

How are you doing so far? Would you consider yourself a biblical church member? Are you truly committed to corporate worship? I'm not asking if you attend church on Sunday mornings. Rather, I'm asking if you deliberately engage in individual worship from your heart. And, do you deliberately join in corporate worship with and for the benefit of others? If so, you get the hallmark, the stamp of divine approval. That's part of what it means to be a biblical church member.

What if you have fallen short? Repent of your half-hearted worship and determine from this day forward to genuinely change. What does that look like? I encourage you to take three practical steps. First, re-read this chapter and study the Scriptures we have worked through. Second, make a few notes on what you have learned and place them in your Bible. For the next few months, on Saturday night or Sunday morning, review them. Finally, ask the Holy Spirit to make you a true worshiper with God's people. My prayer is that God will extend His grace to you to become a true worshiper with His people.

Hallmark #2

Service

As each one has received a special gift, employ it in serving one another as good stewards of the manifold grace of God. Whoever speaks, is to do so as one who is speaking the utterances of God; whoever serves is to do so as one who is serving by the strength which God supplies; so that in all things God may be glorified through Jesus Christ, to whom belongs the glory and dominion forever and ever. Amen.

1 PETER 4:10–11

FIVE

Service in the Church

Jesus Christ is in a league of His own as the greatest servant this world has ever seen. In fact, He stated that the primary purpose of His incarnation was to serve (Matt. 20:28; Phil. 2:7). In the Gospel of Mark, Jesus taught His disciples a lesson about true greatness in His kingdom (10:35–45). To illustrate His point, Jesus used Himself as the supreme example of self-giving love and sacrificial service to others.

At the climax of the lesson Jesus said, "For even the Son of Man did not come to be served, but to serve, and to give His life a ransom for many" (10:45). The Greek word for "served" means "to do, or render a service." It was frequently used in the ancient world for waiting tables, and eventually came to be associated with various acts of lowly service. Jesus' point was simply this: true greatness in His kingdom is defined by serving others and giving yourself as the slave of others.

In what way did Jesus, the Son of Man, demonstrate a life of service to others? As the eternal Son of God, He took on human flesh to offer Himself up as a substitutionary atonement for sins (John 1:14; Rom. 3:21–26). He added to Himself human nature in order to lay down His life as a ransom, a sacrificial death, for many, for all those who would ever repent from their sins and call Him Lord (Rom 10:9–10).

The goal of the Christian life is ultimately to become like Jesus Christ, for His glory. That means every Christian must be committed to imitating our Lord in every aspect of life. If we're going to be like Christ, like Him, we must serve His people. The second hallmark of a biblical church member is *service*. How are Christians supposed to carry out this task? Thankfully, Christ has given us His plan for our service in the local church.

Christ's Plan for Service

The letter to the Ephesians records Paul's explanation of the eternal plan of God as it relates to Christ and His church. The first three chapters capture the rich theology and doctrine of that plan. When chapter four begins, Paul explains how Christians should respond to the spiritual blessings they have received in Christ (Eph. 1:3). Paul writes, "Therefore, I, the prisoner of the Lord, implore you to walk in a manner worthy of the calling with which you have been called" (Eph. 4:1). In the subsequent verses, Paul explains how believers must live in light of what God has done for them through Christ. Christians serve Christ by serving one another in Christ's church. Ephesians 4:7–13 says:

> To each one of us grace was given according to the measure of Christ's gift. Therefore it says, 'When He ascended on

high, He led captive a host of captives, and He gave gifts to men.' (Now this *expression*, 'He ascended,' what does it mean except that He also had descended into the lower parts of the earth? He who descended is Himself also He who ascended far above all the heavens, so that He might fill all things.) And He gave some *as* apostles, and some *as* prophets, and some *as* evangelists, and some *as* pastors and teachers, for the equipping of the saints for the work of service, to the building up of the body of Christ; until we all attain to the unity of the faith, and of the knowledge of the Son of God, to a mature man, to the measure of the stature which belongs to the fullness of Christ.

In these remarkable verses we discover Christ's plan for His church, how it should function. First, Christ sovereignly distributes spiritual gifts to each member of His church. Ephesians 4:7 says, "To each one of us grace was given according to the measure of Christ's gift."

Second, Christ appoints the leaders of each church. Paul writes, "He gave some *as* apostles, and some *as* prophets, and some *as* evangelists, and some *as* pastors and teachers" (Eph. 4:11). This is a list of gifted leaders that God has given, in Christ, to the church.

Paul uses the expression "pastors and teachers" to identify one particular office within the church, that of teaching shepherds. The office of "pastor-teacher" is also described in the New Testament as "overseer" and "elder" (Acts 20:28; 1 Pet. 5:1–2). In fact, all five terms are used interchangeably in the New Testament to describe the elders of a church. Both Acts 20 and 1 Timothy 5 describe a plurality of elders who shepherded the church in Ephesus, some of whom were paid and others were not (1 Tim. 5:17).

Third, the leaders of the church are to equip the members to do the ministry of the church. Those in church leadership are called to equip the people of God (4:12). The primary role of the elders isn't to do the ministry. Rather, it's to equip believers to do the work of ministry. If the pastors or elders do all the work, that represents a skewed view of Christ's plan for the church. A healthy, biblical model is for the elders to equip the saints for the work of ministry.

Fourth, the members do the ministry of the church. Church leaders ought to be equipping the members of the church "for the work of service" (4:12). The Greek word for "service" can be used for any kind of service. For example, in Acts 6:4, it's used for ministering the Word. In Luke 10:40 and Acts 6:2, it's used for preparing and serving food. Every member of the church ought to be involved in service at some level, from the public proclamation of God's Word from the pulpit in corporate worship, to menial acts of service across the church. The point is everyone ought to be serving!

Fifth, following Christ's plan results in the spiritual growth of the church. Paul refers to this as the "building up of the body of Christ" (4:12). As God's plan for the church unfolds and as we faithfully serve one another, the church grows spiritually. Service, then, isn't peripheral. Instead, service is integral to Christ's plan for His church, including the spiritual growth of every brother and sister in Christ. Therefore, if you are a follower of Jesus Christ, His plan for you is to serve in His church, and to do so faithfully.

Gifts for Service

Not only has Christ given us His plan and the framework for our service in the church, but He has also given each individual believer the means to do so. Christ has graciously given every believer a unique spiritual giftedness to use in serving one another in the church. In

Peter's first epistle, he explains the concept of using our spiritual gifts in the church. He writes:

> As each one has received a *special* gift, employ it in serving one another as good stewards of the manifold grace of God. Whoever speaks, *is to do so* as one who is speaking the utterances of God; whoever serves *is to do so* as one who is serving by the strength which God supplies; so that in all things God may be glorified through Jesus Christ, to whom belongs the glory and dominion forever and ever. Amen. (1 Pet. 4:10–11)

Spiritual gifts are meant to be used for the glory of Jesus Christ and God the Father. Every Christian is called to use his or her gifts with this goal in mind. Peter begins by affirming that all Christians have spiritual gifts (v. 10). To emphasize this point, in Greek Peter places the phrase "As each one" in an emphatic position. He intends to stress that every true Christian has spiritual gifts.

This is the message of the entire New Testament. Romans 12:3 says, "Through the grace given to me I say to everyone among you not to think more highly of himself than he ought to think; but to think so as to have sound judgment, as God has allotted to each a measure of faith. Paul adds in 1 Corinthians 12:7, "To each one is given the manifestation of the Spirit for the common good." Just as every member of your physical body has a function, so does every member of Christ's spiritual body.

It's critical to understand that we aren't the source of our spiritual gifts—God is. Sinclair Ferguson writes, "Spiritual gifts reflect more about the grace of the Giver than they reveal about the gracious condition of the recipient."[1] When Peter says "as each one has received," he intends to show that God alone is the source and giver of every gift.[2] In addition, his use of the past tense ("has received") means that these gifts were given in the past. Both 1 Peter 4:10 and 1 Corinthians 12:13, reveal that spiritual gifts are given at the moment of conversion.

If you are a believer, when you heard gospel of Jesus Christ, the Holy Spirit made you, who were dead in trespasses and sins, alive in Christ—that's regeneration. God used the good news of salvation in Christ to bring your dead soul to life. Once you repented of your sins and believed in Christ, God justified you and declared you righteous before Him. As if that were not enough, He then adopted you into His family as one of His children! At that same moment, the Holy Spirit gave you spiritual gifts. In fact, Peter says, "Each one has received a *special* gift." The Greek word for "gift" is *charisma* which literally means "a gift of grace." In the same way that your salvation was not earned or merited, neither is the Holy Spirit's gift to you. It's just an expression of God's grace and His unmerited favor toward you. Thomas Schreiner says, "Believers cannot boast about the gift they have, for otherwise they contradict its gracious character, thinking that somehow they merit its bestowal. The gifts are manifestations of God's grace in its various forms."[3]

When Peter speaks of this "special gift," he's undoubtedly referring to the New Testament concept of spiritual gifts. Today, there's a massive amount of confusion about the meaning and function of spiritual gifts. Simply stated, a spiritual gift is a unique capacity for

---

1 Sinclair Ferguson, *The Holy Spirit*, Contours of Christian Theology (Downers Grove, IL: InterVarsity, 1996), 209.

2 The aorist tense of the Greek verb *lambanō* (λαμβάνω; "received") should be understood as a divine passive.

3 Thomas Schreiner, *1, 2 Peter, Jude*, New American Commentary (Nashville, TN: B&H, 2003), 214.

service given to every true Christian. The New Testament presents two basic categories of gifts.

The first is temporary sign gifts, also known as the miraculous gifts. The New Testament describes ten temporary, miraculous gifts that can be sub-divided into two categories: The gifts for *revelation* were apostle, prophecy, distinguishing of spirits, word of wisdom, and word of knowledge. Because the New Testament hadn't been written, God used these gifts to reveal His truth to the church. The gifts for *confirmation* were miracles, healings, languages ("tongues"), and the interpretation of languages ("tongues"). These gifts were signs or identification markers of the true apostles in the first century. 2 Corinthians 12:12 says, "The signs of a true apostle were performed among you with all perseverance, by signs and wonders and miracles" (cf. Rom. 15:19; Heb. 2:1–4).

The purpose of the sign gifts was to authenticate the apostles and the message they preached. In the apostles' case, their message was authentic revelation from God—the true Word of God (1 Thess. 2:13). This type of revelation continued until the written Word was completed in the late 90s AD. Then, that written Word, which was authored by the apostles and their associates, became self-authenticating by the power of the Holy Spirit. From that time forward, because the written Word of God was complete, there was no longer a need for the miraculous sign gifts.[4]

The second category of gifts is the permanent edifying gifts, found in Romans 12:6–8, 1 Corinthians 12:8–10; 28, and Ephesians 4:11. In total there are eight different permanent edifying gifts: teach-

---

4 For a further defense of the cessation of the miraculous gifts, see the two-part sermon series "A Case for Cessationism" that I preached at Countryside Bible Church in 2014. You can find both the audio and transcripts here: https://countrysidebible.org/media or https://thewordunleashed.org/sermons/. In addition, I also preached a similar message at the Strange Fire Conference in 2013. That sermon was also titled "A Case for Cessationism." You can view it here: https://www.youtube.com/watch?v=900z-J4RnwE&t=11s.

ing, exhortation, evangelism, pastor-teacher, helps, giving, administration and mercy. Those eight, however, may not be exhaustive; they may simply represent the potential diversity of the Holy Spirit's gifts. Regardless, the eight permanent edifying gifts are like a divine palette. It isn't as if every believer gets only one gift. Rather, the Holy Spirit uses the eight permanent gifts and blends them as He sees fit for each believer. You have been given a special giftedness uniquely crafted by the Holy Spirit!

Discovering Your Gifts

At this point a key question usually arises: "How can I discover my gift?" That's a valid question for those of us who want to serve the Lord in the way He equipped us. So, how do you find out? First, go to the Scripture: read, study, and meditate on 1 Peter 4, 1 Corinthians 12, and Romans 12. Seek to understand what the Scriptures say, and pray for wisdom and direction. Second, seek the input and guidance of spiritually mature people around you who can help you understand what you are, and aren't, gifted to do, especially from your elders. Third, just get busy serving in the life of the church! We all tend to gravitate toward the areas of our gifts.

Think about your own physical body. So many of the functions of your physical body are involuntary. You don't think about them, the members just do their part. Your pancreas didn't have to take a three-page personality survey to determine what its gifts are and how it fits into the body. Thankfully, our bodies work because God made them to work.

The same is true of our spiritual giftedness. Don't spend time worrying about what your gift is. Rather, get involved in the life of the church. And as that happens, you will gravitate toward areas of service that correspond with your giftedness. To whatever extent you might be confused about, or questioning, your gifts, the Holy Spirit will direct you through His Word and the wise guidance of the people of the church to help you. With time you will begin to exercise your gifts in the church, filling the role for which God gifted you. Get busy, get involved, and serve!

Serving Others

After Peter calls believers to understand their special giftedness, he then tells them to "employ it in serving" (1 Pet. 4:10). These four English words actually translate one Greek word *diakonountes*, the verb form of the noun *deacon* (*diakonos*). It's used for the office of deacon in the New Testament (1 Tim. 3:8–13), but it's also used for general, selfless service. Peter exhorts his readers to serve one another with the gifts they have received from the Spirit. Your spiritual gift is to be the primary channel through which you minister to Christ and His people. 1 Corinthians 12:7 says, "To each one is given the manifestation of the Spirit *for the common good*" (emphasis added). Paul simply says you have been gifted for the benefit of others. Robert L. Thomas writes, "[Spiritual gifts] must be seen, heard, or in some manner experienced by at least one person other than the gifted one. The Giver never intended any spiritual gift for private purposes, and to the extent that one uses a gift that way, he or she abuses that given ability."[5]

By God's grace I've been gifted to teach. And when I study and prepare to teach, I benefit more than those who hear me, in the sense that I cannot teach everything I learned—I'm grateful the Lord uses my gift for my own soul. However, we're called primarily to use our gifts for the common good; I hope and pray God has been pleased to use my gift to that end. In 1 Corinthians 14:26 Paul writes, "What

---

5 Robert L. Thomas, *Understanding Spiritual Gifts*, rev. ed. (Grand Rapids: Kregel,1999), 27.

is *the outcome* then, brethren? When you assemble, each one has a psalm, has a teaching, has a revelation, has a tongue, has an interpretation. Let all things be done for edification." From the beginning, all spiritual gifts were intended to edify and build up the entire body of Christ.

I want this truth to resonate deep within your soul. God has given you—if you are a true follower of Jesus Christ—a unique blend of special abilities, and He demands that you use them to serve others. Christians have a unique duty and responsibility to faithfully serve others in the church.

How should we handle this type of responsibility? Peter writes, "as good stewards" (1 Pet. 4:10). The Greek word for "steward" literally means "house manager." In the first century, this word was used for the slave who was responsible for managing his master's property. We aren't owners of our giftedness; we're merely managers.

Peter describes our giftedness as "the manifold grace of God" (1 Pet. 4:10). The word "manifold" means many-colored and often speaks of variety. Corporately, there's a great variety of giftedness represented in every church. Praise God for His providential arrangement of that! Individually, each of us has a mixture of gifts; may God help us use them as stewards, with humble hearts. We're merely slaves using our Master's resources to accomplish His work. R.C. Sproul writes, "We are to be good stewards of the plentiful, abundant grace of God for the edification of the body of Christ.... We have a responsibility to be stewards of God's gifts...God has given you and me grace, which is a gift, but with the gift comes a responsibility."[6]

---

6 R.C. Sproul, *1–2 Peter: An Expositional Commentary* (Sanford, FL: Reformation Trust, 2019), 138.

SIX

Speaking and Serving Gifts

We have already established that the New Testament divides spiritual gifts into two categories (temporary miraculous gifts and permanent edifying gifts). Peter further categorizes the permanent edifying gifts by dividing them into two groups: speaking and serving (1 Pet. 4:11). Peter argues that all believers either have a speaking gift, a serving gift, or a combination. He writes, "Whoever speaks, *is to do so* as one who is speaking the utterances of God; whoever serves *is to do so* as one who is serving by the strength which God supplies; so that in all things God may be glorified through Jesus Christ, to whom belongs the glory and dominion forever and ever. Amen" (1 Pet. 4:11).

Speaking Gifts

Peter identifies speaking gifts with the phrase "whoever speaks" (4:11). The Greek word for "speaks" (*lalei*) is primarily used in two ways. First, it's often used for public speaking, the public teaching of God's

Word. Second, it's used for private conversations. Peter intentionally selects this word to include all speaking gifts, everything from the public proclamation of Scripture in the corporate assembly, to private exhortation. You may be a public speaker, or perhaps you have the gift of exhortation and are able to privately encourage, challenge, and counsel someone towards Christlikeness.

How should you exercise your speaking gift? Peter writes, "Whoever speaks is to do so as one who is speaking the utterances of God" (4:11). The English word "utterances" isn't a word we use frequently. In classical Greek, the word for "utterances" is used to identify a word or message from a deity. It's used the same way in both the Septuagint (the Greek translation of the Hebrew Old Testament) and the New Testament. In the Septuagint, it's used to translate the common expression "the Word of the Lord." The New Testament authors sometimes use this word when they speak of the Old Testament. For example, Paul refers to the Old Testament as "the oracles of God" (Rom. 3:2). The Greek word for "oracles" is the same word translated "utterances." In other words, utterances are the oracles of God. Peter is simply saying, if you have a speaking gift, you are to speak as if you are speaking the very words of God.

That leads to two primary points of application for those with speaking gifts. First, our content should only be the Word of God. As a preacher of God's Word, apart from the Bible, I don't have anything to say that's worth anyone's time. I'm unable to personally offer anything of value and worth. I'm called to preach and speak the Word of God, the utterances of God. The same is true of anyone who teaches publicly or privately.

This is a reminder to beware of those who say they have teaching gifts—whether a television preacher or a pastor down the street. If their teaching is all about themselves, and the message they offer comes from their own mind, not the Scripture, they are abusing their giftedness (if they have it at all), because the one who speaks is to speak the oracles of God.

The second primary point of application is to teach God's Word with authority. That means to unashamedly teach and preach the Bible as the very words of God, and to present it as the final authority in everything it addresses. That's the job of everyone who has a speaking gift: deliver the authoritative oracles of God to God's people. That's why Paul says to Titus, "These things speak and exhort and reprove with all authority. Let no one disregard you" (Titus 2:15). The teaching of God's Word by those gifted to do so isn't to be a conversation—it's a proclamation of the very words of God.

Serving Gifts

The second category of spiritual gifts that Peter addresses is serving gifts. He introduces this category with the phrase "whoever serves" (4:11). This includes every gift that isn't a speaking gift. If you don't have a speaking gift, you have serving gifts. Peter goes on to make a remarkable statement about serving gifts: "Whoever serves *is to do so* as one who is serving by the strength which God supplies" (4:11). God supplies the necessary strength to successfully use serving gifts. We must rely not on our own strength, but rather on God's adequate supply of strength. The Greek word for "supplies" means to richly or lavishly supply. It was often used in the ancient world for leading a chorus or group of performers. Peter's point is that God will give an abundance of strength to those with serving gifts so they can serve others faithfully.

Again, by God's grace and the sovereign decision of His Spirit I believe I also have the gift of administration. Through the years I've had the opportunity to use this gift in overseeing several organizations. I can tell you from experience that it's easy for those with serving gifts to begin to depend solely on their own strength and resources. Peter says, "Don't do that!" Don't approach your service with the attitude that you have this handled. Don't rely on yourself. Don't rely on your own experience, creativity or hard work. Instead, remind yourself that you need God's strength to serve effectively, and ask Him for help to do so. Those with serving gifts who depend on their own strength often burn out.

The Reality of Your Service

On the Tuesday before Jesus' crucifixion, He delivered a sermon commonly titled "The Olivet Discourse." In this sermon He gives a detailed account of the future judgment that will happen at the end of the seven-year Tribulation period. When Christ returns at His Second Coming, He will righteously judge every person who survives the Tribulation. Theologians call this judgment the "Judgment of Nations," but in reality it's a judgment of individuals. Matthew records Jesus' words:

> When the Son of Man comes in His glory, and all the angels with Him, then He will sit on His glorious throne. All the nations will be gathered before Him; and He will separate them from one another, as the shepherd separates the sheep from the goats; and He will put the sheep on His right, and the goats on the left.

> Then the King will say to those on His right, 'Come, you who are blessed of My Father, inherit the kingdom prepared for you from the foundation of the world. For I was hungry, and you gave Me *something* to eat; I was thirsty, and you gave Me

something to drink; I was a stranger, and you invited Me in; naked, and you clothed Me; I was sick, and you visited Me; I was in prison, and you came to Me.' Then the righteous will answer Him, 'Lord, when did we see You hungry, and feed You, or thirsty, and give You *something* to drink? And when did we see You a stranger, and invite You in, or naked, and clothe You? When did we see You sick, or in prison, and come to You?' The King will answer and say to them, 'Truly I say to you, to the extent that you did it to one of these brothers of Mine, *even* the least *of them*, you did it to Me.' (Matt. 25:31–40)

This passage gives us great insight into how Christ views service to Him and His people.

When the Son of Man returns to the earth at the Second Coming, He will gather the nations and "separate them from one another, as a shepherd separates the sheep from the goats" (v. 32). How do you become one of Christ's sheep? It isn't because of good works, but because God the Father determined to call you into the kingdom that He prepared for you before the foundation of the world: "The King will say to those on His right, 'Come, you who are blessed of my Father, inherit the kingdom prepared for you from the foundation of the world'" (v. 34). You became a sheep and you will be in the kingdom, solely because of God's sovereign grace, based entirely on the righteous life, subsitutionary death, and victorious resurrection of Jesus Christ.

Although salvation is all of grace, Jesus highlights the importance of good works as evidence of genuine faith. He says,

For I was hungry, and you gave Me *something* to eat; I was

thirsty, and you gave Me *something* to drink; I was a stranger, and you invited Me in; naked, and you clothed Me; I was sick, and you visited Me; I was in prison, and you came to Me. (v. 35–36)

Did you notice Jesus' use of the pronouns "I" and "you"? Jesus is saying to the believers who survived the Tribulation, that the good works they did for others were ultimately done to Him. Then believers will say, "Lord, when did we see You hungry, and feed You, or thirsty, and give You *something* to drink? And when did we see You a stranger, and invite You in, or naked, and clothe You? When did we see You sick, or in prison, and come to You?" (v. 37–39). Jesus says, "Truly I say to you, to the extent that you did it to one of these brothers of Mine, *even* the least *of them*, you did it to Me" (v. 40).

In context, "brothers of Mine" refers to all those who have believed in Jesus as Savior and Lord. Of course, we're called to be compassionate and gracious and to perform acts of mercy toward the unbelieving world. However, here Jesus is specifically talking about believers doing these things, in His name, for other believers. When you serve another believer with the right heart, you are serving our Lord Jesus Christ. What a staggering reality! Our Lord sees and takes note of every act of service we do for another brother or sister in Christ.

And at the Judgment, He will acknowledge and praise that act of service as if you literally did it to Him. The author of Hebrews says, "God is not unjust so as to forget your work and the love which you have shown toward His name, in having ministered and in still ministering to the saints" (Heb. 6:10). Matthew Henry writes, "Good works and labor proceeding from love to God are commendable; and what is done to any in the name of God shall not go unrewarded.

What is done to the saints, as such, God takes as done to himself."[1]

One of the primary ways to show your love for Christ is by ministering to the people in His church. The opposite is equally true: failure to minister to those in the church is to demonstrate a lack of love for Jesus. In fact, in John 21:15–17 when Jesus restored Peter, He asked him three times, "Peter, do you love Me?" Each time Peter answered by saying, "Yes, Lord, I love You." Each time Jesus responds by saying, "Tend My lambs," and "Shepherd My sheep." The context of John 21 is primarily about Jesus' commissioning of Peter and the apostles. However, the command and principle is true for every Christian. If you want to show your love for Jesus Christ, love His people.

Occasionally people say to me, "Tom, I love Christ, but I don't need the church." That type of statement is utterly incongruous. It's impossible to love the Head of the church, Jesus Christ, and not love His body, the church. You cannot love the Father of our Lord Jesus Christ and not love His children.

Would You Receive the Hallmark?

Are you regularly serving the people of your church? Would you receive a hallmark for faithful service in Christ's church? Would God give you the divine stamp of approval? If not, how do you begin to obey in this area? First, understand that the Lord has equipped and commanded you to serve His church. Second, commit to obey Him; tell Him, "Lord, I'm done making excuses; I'm going to get involved; I'm going to serve You in the church." Third, discover the needs of your church and how you can help in those areas. Again, get busy, get involved, and serve!

---

1 Matthew Henry, *A Commentary on the Whole Bible*, vol. 6, Acts to Revelation (Old Tappan, NJ: Fleming H. Revell), 914.

My prayer is that God will give you a desire to love and serve Him by loving and serving His people.

Hallmark #3

Fellowship

They were continually devoting themselves to the apostles' teaching and to fellowship, to the breaking of bread and to prayer.

ACTS 2:42

SEVEN

Fellowship in the Church

In the nineteenth century, David Dickson was ordained as an elder in the Free New North Church in Scotland where he served for three decades. He was known as a faithful shepherd and a diligent student of Scripture. Both his knowledge of God's Word and his experience as an elder, compelled him to write the classic *The Elder and His Work*, a short treatise about elders and their duties in Christ's church.

As he began thinking through the biblical teaching on fellowship and many churches neglect of it, he wrote, "One great evil existing in our congregations, especially in large towns, is that many of the members don't know or take an interest in each other. It is a blessed hope that we shall recognize our friends in heaven, but let us begin by first recognizing them on earth."[1]

What Dickson wrote over 150 years ago still rings true today. The church desperately needs to rediscover what it means to participate

---

1 David Dickson, *The Elder and His Work* (Phillipsburg, NJ: P&R, 2004), 108.

in biblical fellowship. The New Testament places a great emphasis on fellowship in the context of the local church. Therefore, the third hallmark of a biblical church member is fellowship.

Unfortunately, we're all guilty of misusing the word "fellowship." When Christians get together for donuts and coffee, or activities in general, we tend to call it fellowship. There's a sense in which that's true, if you understand what is really happening. However, fellowship is much more than getting together.

The Greek word for fellowship is *koinonia*. It means to share a common life with one another. During the time of Jesus and the apostles, the form of Greek spoken was *Koine* Greek, which means common Greek. It was considered the common language of the people—marketplace Greek—because it was so widely and commonly shared. In the same way, *koinonia* or fellowship means to share in common. Remember how J.R.R. Tolkien uses the word *fellowship* in his book *The Fellowship of the Ring*. It refers to the small group who bound themselves together with Frodo Baggins to destroy the Ring of Power. That group had a partnership with one another—they were in the fellowship.

That's how *koinonia* is most often used in the New Testament. It describes a fellowship and partnership with God (and Christ) and with other believers. To be in partnership with God and Christ means that we have come to know God as our Father and His Son as our Savior and Lord. Paul writes in 1 Corinthians 1:9, "God is faithful, through whom you were called into fellowship with His Son, Jesus Christ our Lord." The apostles understood this reality when they proclaimed "indeed our fellowship is with the Father, and with His Son Jesus Christ" (1 John 1:3). Believers are no longer dead in their sins and enemies of God (Rom. 5:10; Eph. 2:1–3). Rather, we have been made alive in Christ and brought into a unique fellowship with him (Eph. 2:4–5). Now that we're in Christ, our lives must reflect that fellowship.

Believers have also been brought into fellowship with one another. That doesn't mean we necessarily have a lot in common and have the same interests. The truth is, just like those who bound themselves together in *The Fellowship of the Ring*, Christians often don't have much in common naturally.

Consider the church in Philippi. The founding members were Lydia, a successful Greek business woman, a former demon-possessed slave girl who had worked as a fortune teller, and a jailer. They came from very different walks of life and had absolutely nothing in common, by the world's standards. However, Philippians 1:5 says they had a "partnership in the gospel" (ESV). The Greek word for "partnership" is *koinonia*, and could be translated as "participation" or "fellowship." The believers in Philippi were united by their shared commitment to Jesus Christ. And that's what unites every single believer. True, some of us have common backgrounds and interests, but many of us don't. And that's okay! What binds us together is not our demographics, but the fellowship of the gospel. This is the fellowship and partnership we have been brought into through Christ.

The book of Acts records how the early church actively engaged in fellowship. At the conclusion of Peter's sermon at Pentecost, we're told that 3000 people repented from their sins, believed the gospel, and were baptized (Acts 2:41). The church exponentially grew that morning from 120 people to just over 3000! What did the church do from there? Acts 2:42 says, "They were continually devoting themselves to the apostles' teaching and to fellowship, to the breaking of bread and to prayer." The church committed themselves to four priorities: to the apostles' teaching, to fellowship, to the breaking of bread (the Lord's Table), and to prayer. Fellowship was one of the four priorities of the early church.

But in Acts 2, "fellowship" isn't used in the normal, relational sense, but refers to an activity. In other words, believers are to be continually devoted to the activity of fellowship. What exactly does that mean? In context, we learn that fellowship is the sharing of our lives with one another because of the relationship we have in the fellowship of the gospel. It's the practical outcome of the fellowship we belong to. Because we have fellowship in Christ, we engage in fellowship by sharing our lives with one another.

The Activity of Fellowship

The New Testament gives four basic expressions of the activity of fellowship. In other words, how Christians are to *do* fellowship. First, we share a common worship. Acts 2:42 describes believers hearing the teaching of the truth ("apostles' doctrine"), participating in the Lord's Table ("breaking of bread"), and approaching the Lord in prayer ("prayer"). That's a clear picture of the regulative principle at work. The early church was devoted to the activity of fellowship in corporate worship. J. A. Alexander writes,

> The infant church was constantly engaged in mutual communion [fellowship], both by joint repasts and sacramental feasts and charitable distribution....Its whole organization and condition was as yet that of a family, so that all their acts performed in common partook more or less of a religious character.[2]

We must mimic the early church and the fellowship they had in

---

2 J. A. Alexander, *Acts*, Geneva Series of Commentaries (Carlisle, PA: Banner of Truth, 1991), 90–91.

worship.

Second, we fellowship by sharing a common life. This is actually the primary focus of fellowship in Acts 2:42. Those who belonged to the first church in Jerusalem "were continually devoting themselves to fellowship," which simply means they shared their lives with one another. What does that look like? Acts 2:44 says that "all those who had believed were *together*" (emphasis added). They were continuously with one another. Verse 46 says, "Day by day continuing with one mind in the temple, and breaking bread from house to house, they were taking their meals together with gladness and sincerity of heart." The early church's practice was to fellowship daily with one another.

Speaking about the first century church, B. B. Warfield writes,

[They were] sharers on the one hand in a common hope and life, and on the other in a common contempt and persecution; ministered to by a common apostolic body, professing a common faith, partakers in common spiritual gifts, [and] practicing a common peculiar morality.[3]

The first century Christians were unwavering in their commitment to doing life together. Warfield adds that their common life was visible "from one end of the empire to the other."[4] Christians are members of one body, the body of Christ. We're members of one family, the family of God. And that's true of all believers. Therefore, we share a common life.

One of the chief expressions of our fellowship is the sharing of our lives, especially our spiritual lives. How does sharing our com-

---

3 Benjamin Breckinridge Warfield, *Selected Shorter Writings of Benjamin B. Warfield*, vol. 1 (Phillipsburg, NJ: P&R, 1970), 300.
4 Ibid., 300.

mon spiritual life happen? It happens when we're side by side. In other words, there's a fellowship that happens even when believers are sitting next to each other in corporate worship. But it also happens face to face when we sit down across from each other for a meal, or a home Bible study, or a conversation at church.

We must pursue both side-by-side and face-to-face sharing of our spiritual lives. Practically, get together with other believers for coffee or dinner. Have someone over to your home. Get involved in a ministry where you can get to know believers on a more intimate level. Attend a Sunday school class where you can sit around a table with a consistent group of people week after week. Actively seek to get to know them so you can learn more about their lives, and they can learn more about yours. Somehow, you have to engage in sharing common spiritual life with other Christians.

Third, we fellowship by engaging in mutual care. This expression of fellowship requires that you know Christians well enough to be able to practice the "one anothers" of the New Testament. Think of the places in the New Testament where the words "one another" are used to describe the attitudes and behaviors that believers should have towards one another. Jesus said to the disciples in John 13:34, "A new commandment I give to you, that you *love one another*, even as I have loved you, that you also love one another." Paul writes in Galatians 5:13, "You were called to freedom, brethren; only *do* not *turn* your freedom into an opportunity for the flesh, but through love *serve one another*." Later in Galatians he adds, "*Bear one another's burdens*, and thereby fulfill the law of Christ" (Gal. 6:2). Our Lord's half-brother, James, writes, "Therefore, *confess your sins to one another*, and *pray for one another* so that you may be healed. The effective prayer of a righteous man can accomplish much" (Jas. 5:16). This is just a representative sample of the many "one anothers" in the New Testament.

The point is that mutual care can only happen when you know people well enough to be in their lives. The New Testament church modeled this well: "All those who had believed were together and had all things in common; and they *began* selling their property and possessions and were sharing them with all, as anyone might have need" (Acts 2:44–45). That's a perfect representation of what the New Testament church looked like. Not only were the early Christians working together, but they were also sharing with believers in need.

This isn't some kind of "Christian communism." Rather, these Christians were graciously giving up their own property out of mutual love and care for one another. They held everything they owned loosely, so they could benefit and bless other Christians. They were quick to share what they had to meet the needs of others. Acts 4:32 says, "And the congregation of those who believed were of one heart and soul; and not one *of them* claimed that anything belonging to him was his own, but all things were considered common property to them." This congregation didn't cling to ownership of their possessions; instead, they truly believed all that they had was the Lord's and used it to help others.

I Corinthians 12:25 says that God has ordered the church such that "there may be no division in the body, but *that* the members may have the same care for one another." Christ's people are called to lovingly care for one another. John asks, "But whoever has the world's goods, and sees his brother in need and closes his heart against him, how does the love of God abide in him? Little children, let us not love with word or with tongue, but in deed and truth" (I John 3:17–18). In other words, how can you have this world's goods and see your brother in need and not act to meet those needs? How does the love of Christ abide in you if you aren't driven to meet the needs of other people? Mutual care is imperative to biblical fellowship.

Fourth, we fellowship through mutual edification. Romans 15:2 says, "Each of us is to please his neighbor for his good, to his edification." The word "edification" simply means to build up spiritually. In context, Paul is instructing Christians to be sensitive with issues of conscience. Believers must handle issues of conscience for the sake of their neighbor, to edify and build him up. The writer of Hebrews speaks of this when he writes,

> Let us consider how to stimulate one another to love and good deeds, not forsaking our own assembling together, as is the habit of some, but encouraging *one another*; and all the more as you see the day drawing near. (Heb. 10:24–25)

These verses teach that believers must regularly assemble, so that we can "stimulate one another to love and good deeds." That's the equivalent of building one another up.

How often do you attend church on the Lord's Day for worship and think, "I'm here to help stimulate others to love and good deeds?" Do you, by your interactions, stimulate other Christians to love Christ more, to love other Christians more, and to do good deeds? That's biblical fellowship. That's mutual edification.

Paul makes a remarkable statement in Romans 1:11–12:

> I long to see you so that I may impart some spiritual gift to you, that you may be established; that is, that I may be encouraged together with you *while* among you, each of us by the other's faith, both yours and mine.

Even though Paul was an apostle and had been a Christian for over thirty years by the time he wrote Romans, he expressed his desire to be with the Christians in Rome. He longed for their encouragement and to be built up in the faith. Paul knew that God uses the fellowship of believers to strengthen one another—regardless of our gifts and maturity.

The Practice of Fellowship

Maybe you haven't understood that you need the fellowship of other Christians. The reality is God uses fellowship with believers to strengthen and encourage us. If you haven't been committed to fellowship, and the Holy Spirit has convicted you through this study of your need for it, consider the following practical suggestions to help you get on track.

First, change your mindset about the church. The culture's consumer mentality has leaked into the church and has done severe damage. It promotes a type of Christianity that focuses primarily on a person's personal relationship with God without any sense of belonging or obligation to the church, the larger body of Christ. The New Testament knows nothing of a genuine believer unattached to and uninvolved with a local body of believers. If you are a Christian nomad who just wanders into different churches but never commits to one, you are sinning against Jesus Christ. And you are sinning against His body.

You have to remove those unbiblical concepts from your mind, and allow the Scripture to reshape your thinking about the purpose of the church. You are an active, functioning member of a body—Christ's body (Eph. 5:30). In addition, as a son or daughter in Christ, you are a member of a family.

Second, connect with a smaller group. Take the initiative to connect with a smaller group of believers in your church so that you can practice fellowship. Join a Sunday school class or a midweek home group. Get involved in a men's or women's Bible study. Research the ministries and groups your church offers and get connected with one of them.

Third, actively pursue individual relationships. There are many practical ways to do this. It starts with corporate worship on the Lord's Day. If possible, get to church earlier and stay later. Give yourself opportunities to meet and engage with people before, during, and after corporate worship. Regularly schedule Sunday lunches—it's a great time to reflect on Sunday morning's activities, discuss the life of the church, and share a meal. And a perfect opportunity to get to know other believers on a personal level.

The bottom line is the New Testament commands every Christian to pursue fellowship with other Christians. Not to do so is to disobey Christ and His Word, and to hinder your spiritual development. Resolve to pursue individual relationships, and look for ways to practice real fellowship according to those four expressions.

Would You Receive the Hallmark?

Are you regularly fellowshipping with God's people? Would you receive the hallmark? If you are consistently engaged in common worship with God's people, if you are committed to sharing your life with others, if you are truly caring for your fellow brothers and sisters in Christ, and if you are seeking to build one another up to love Christ and His people more, you receive the divine stamp of approval, you get the hallmark. Regularly participating in true fellowship is part of what it means to be a biblical church member.

What if you failed this test? What steps do you need to take to ensure you are walking in biblical fellowship? As with every sin, you must acknowledge you have missed the mark and resolve to make a legitimate change. What are practical ways to do that? It always begins with Scripture. Read and study the passages in this chapter. Make it your aim to study how the New Testament church participated in biblical fellowship—pattern your life after theirs. Make a list of ways that you can implement authentic fellowship in your life and then actually do them. Finally, pray that the Spirit of God would renew your mind and change your heart to desire biblical fellowship.

My prayer is that God will graciously bring you into greater fellowship with both Christ and His people.

Conclusion

The New Testament provides clear standards for what it means to be a biblical church member. I'm grateful for the clarity of God's Word and that it speaks to what our priorities ought to be in Christ's church. If the church is a priority for Christ—and it is—we must prioritize it just as He does. His standards for the church must be our standards as well.

That means every Christian must be committed to corporate worship on the Lord's Day. We must be resolved to make the Sunday gatherings with God's people the highest priority of our week. Our desire should be to corporately worship God, in truth, by what He has prescribed in Scripture. The assembling of ourselves is absolutely critical as we wait for our Lord's return (Heb. 10:23–25). Not only must our worship be founded in truth, but in spirit. This means we must make a conscious decision to worship and then commit to an ongoing effort to stay engaged.

In addition to corporate worship, Christians must have an unwavering commitment to serve in the church. Christ has given spiritual giftedness to every believer for the purpose of exercising those gifts to serve Him and His people. Whether you have a speaking gift or serving gift, or a combination, Christ intends for you to use those gifts for the spiritual growth of His church. Failure to use your gift is a failure to obey Christ, the Head of the church. Service is essential to Christ's purposes in the church, and His plan includes using your gifts to that end.

Lastly, we must consistently engage in biblical fellowship. Our lives must center in a common life with God's people. We must genuinely care for the brothers and sisters in Christ we stand next to on Sunday. We must invest our time and efforts in building each other up for the sake of Christ and His gospel.

Be honest with yourself: are you a biblical church member? Are you faithfully committed to weekly corporate worship? Are you faithfully serving Christ by serving Him and His people? Are you intentionally engaged in fellowship, in loving and caring for your fellow believers? Those are the three nonnegotiable hallmarks that characterize a biblical church member. My prayer is that God would help every one of us who belongs to Christ's church, to receive Christ's own hallmark—to be stamped as genuine by our Lord Jesus Christ.

Scripture Index

About the Author

Tom Pennington has served as Pastor-Teacher at Countryside Bible Church in Southlake, Texas since 2003. Prior to arriving in Texas, Tom served in various roles at Grace Community Church in Sun Valley, California for 16 years. His ministry at Grace included being an elder, Senior Associate Pastor, and the personal assistant to John MacArthur. Tom was also an adjunct faculty member of The Master's Seminary and served as Managing Director of Grace to You.

In addition to his pastoral role at Countryside, he serves as Dean of the Dallas Distance Location at The Master's Seminary, teaches various seminary courses, and is actively involved internationally in training pastors in expository preaching.

Tom's preaching and teaching ministry at Countryside is featured on The Word Unleashed (thewordunleashed.org).

About The Greater Heritage

Mission

The Greater Heritage is a Christian publishing ministry that equips believers for an abundant life of service, personal spiritual growth and character development.

What We Do

The Greater Heritage publishes original articles, books, Bible studies and church resources. All of its books are made entirely in the USA.

Want to publish with us? Inquire at:

The Greater Heritage
1170 Tree Swallow Dr., Suite 309
Winter Springs, Florida 32708
info@thegreaterheritage.com
www.thegreaterheritage.com

Find more books and our latest catalog online at:

www.thegreaterheritage.com/shop

THE
Greater ✒ Heritage
Christian   *Publishing*

SPREAD THE WORD - SHARE THIS BOOK

If you enjoyed this book, please consider sharing it with others.
There are many ways to share, including...

- Take a photo with the book and post it on your social media page(s).

- Write a review on your blog or on an online store's product page.

- Share a copy with friends and family or buy one as a gift.

- Recommend this book to your circle of influence.

- Follow The Greater Heritage on Twitter: @TGH_Ministries

- Subscribe to our email list at www.thegreaterheritage.com